If Gratitude Were A Color, It Would Be TURQUOISE

Cover design by Sara Young
Back Cover photo by Childers Photography
Front Cover and interior photos by Molly Kuplen Lifestyle Blog and Photo, LLC

ISBN: MENA - If Gratitude Were a Color ---HC > PB. [9/19]
ISBN: 978-1-964794-19-8   1 2 3 4 5 6 7 8 9 10

Printed in the United States of America

If Gratitude Were A Color, It Would Be TURQUOISE

Laura A. Mena

KUDU

The photos in this book are crocheted pieces by Laura A. Mena. She was taught how to crochet at the age of 11 by her Aunt Terry, and it's the gift that has continued to give throughout her life, and her many years of creating.

This book is inspired by God, and dedicated to my beautiful Grandloves,
who continue to show me the world of color through new eyes.

Thank you:

To my husband, my soulmate, who encourages me daily to grow

To my daughters, who are my best friends

To my sons-in-law, who are my best friends' best friends

To my mom, who always brought color into our lives

To my dad, who has always been there for me

To Linda, who has always been a special part of our family

To my sister who encourages me to say "yes"

To my brother, who has always protected me

To my aunt, who has always taught me to think bigger

To my cousins, who are like sisters

To my soul sisters, you know who you are

To the rest of my family and friends who have brought so much color into my life.

CONTENTS

IF JOY WERE A COLOR, IT WOULD BE YELLOW.

The sun is yellow and says
hello to the new day.

So is the warm feeling of
the sun on my face.

Baby chicks are yellow, fluffy, and soft;

Giraffes are yellow with
lovely brown spots.

Yellow are the yolks that I eat in my eggs.

My mom says it's a lucky day to
get a double yolk by chance.

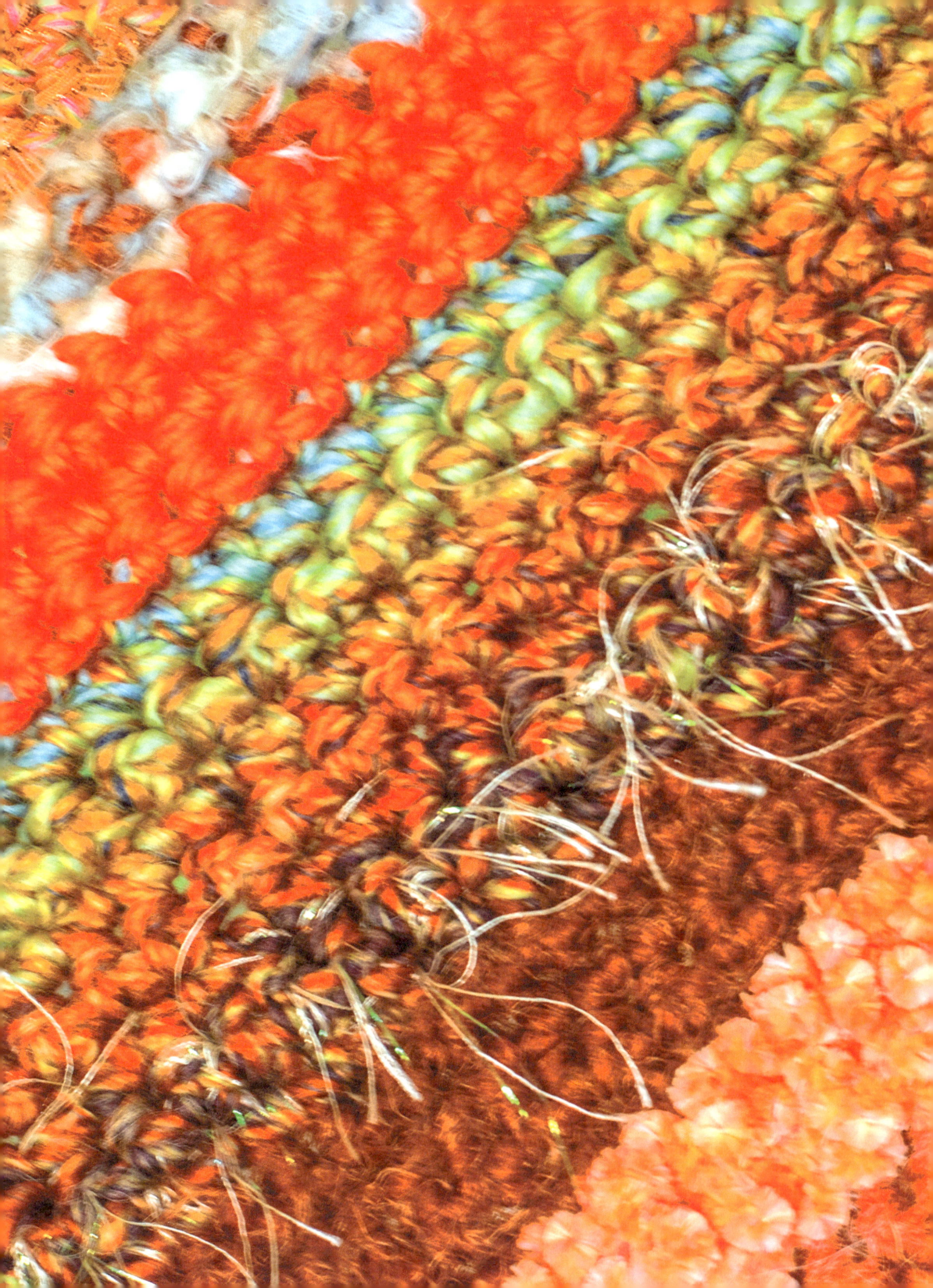

IF HAPPY WERE A COLOR, IT WOULD BE ORANGE.

Orange is like the sunrise
when I wake up early.

Orange like the sherbet I
have occasionally.

Goldfish are usually orange and glittery.

Monarchs are orange, black, and fluttery.

Orange is the tangy and sweet that I feel

When I see an orange that
has been freshly peeled.

IF EXCITEMENT WERE A COLOR, IT WOULD BE RED.

My great-grandmother's lips
were usually this color.

So is the cardinal that reminds me of her.

Red is the feeling when I
eat something spicy.

Like cinnamon sticks, red
hots, or hot tamales.

I usually imagine my heart
being red this way.

So was the Grinch's when it
grew three times that day.

IF LOVE WERE A COLOR, IT WOULD BE PINK.

It can be the color of a
wedding filled with love.

So is the sound of wedding
glasses clinking above.

We find this color in the prettiest of roses.

Sometimes, we see it in bunnies' noses.

Bubble gum is usually pink.

So are babies' bottoms, I think.

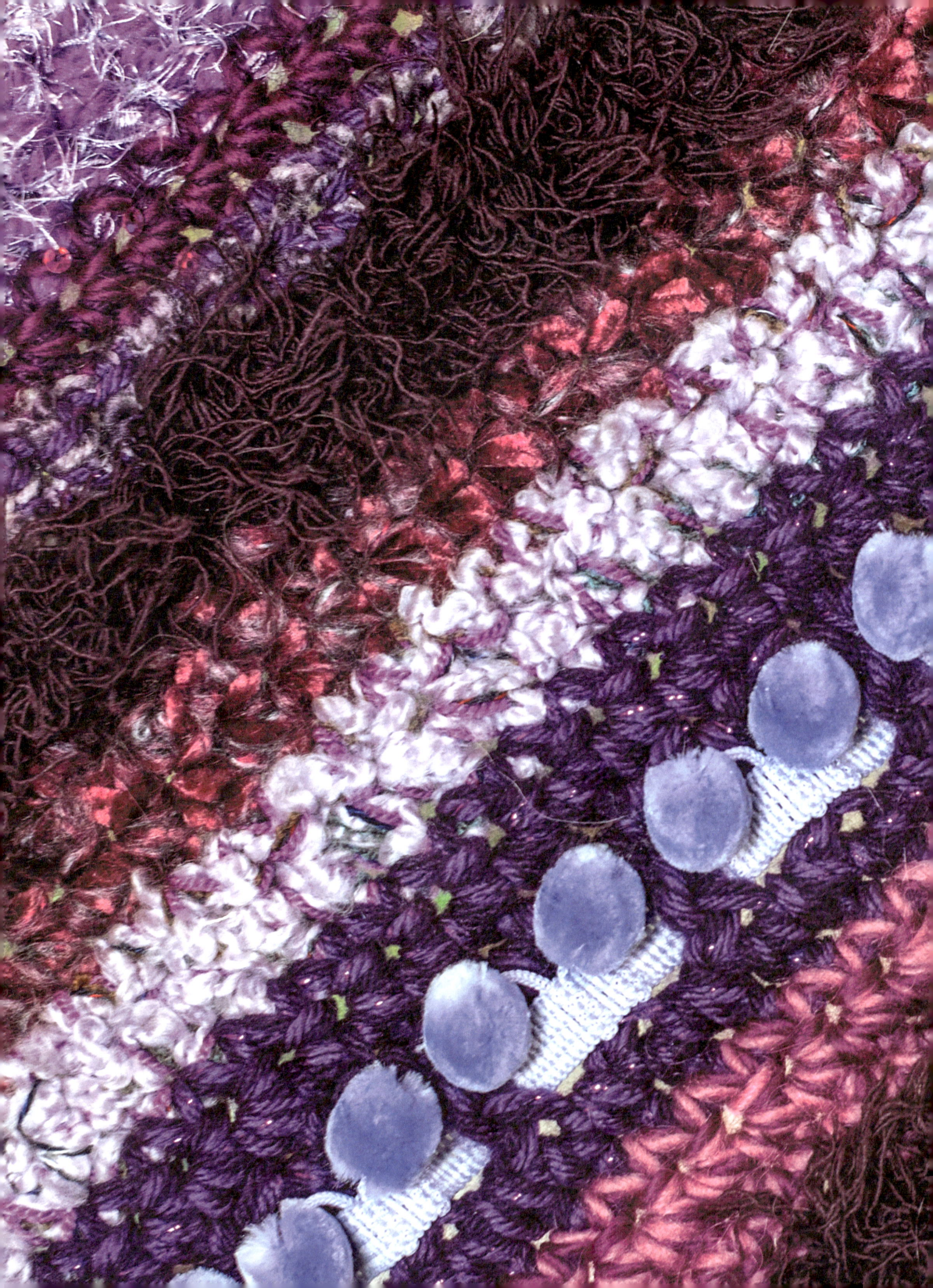

IF CALM WERE A COLOR, IT WOULD BE PURPLE.

We look up to purple mountain majesties.

It's the color of jelly in my sandwiches.

Plums and eggplant are usually this color.

So is the iris and lovely lavender.

Amethyst is a purple stone that
you might see in rings.

I think it's the color of angels' wings.

IF KINDNESS WERE A COLOR, IT WOULD BE BLUE.

Blue like clear, bluebird days.

The color that peeks out
between the sun's rays.

Starfish can sometimes be this color.

It's the feeling I get when I do
something nice for others.

Flowers in the mountains bloom in
shades of this in the summer.

Blueberries are in the muffins
I eat warm with butter.

IF GRATITUDE WERE A COLOR, IT WOULD BE TURQUOISE.

Turquoise, sometimes, is
the sunset at night.

I also see this color in my grandma's eyes.

The ocean can be this shade of blue.

It's usually the color of a swimming pool.

My favorite place where I see this color

Is in a nest of eggs with a robin mother.

IF BEAUTIFUL WERE A COLOR, IT WOULD BE GREEN.

It's the valleys between the
mountain ranges.

The color of a pine tree
that never changes.

Green is the smell of fresh-cut grass.

Sometimes, we drink green
tea from a glass.

It's the first color we see in the spring

Which the sun and the rain help to bring.

IF WARMTH WERE A COLOR, IT WOULD BE BROWN.

It's the color of a baby bunny,

Also, my blanket that is warm and fuzzy.

Chocolate chip cookies are
usually this shade.

So is the feeling when I eat
them freshly made.

Coffee is this color, and my
mom adds cream.

Hot chocolate is, too, with
yummy whipped foam.

IF PEACE WERE A COLOR, IT WOULD BE WHITE.

White is the tissue that
wipes away my tears.

White is the feeling that God is near.

A new sheet of paper is crispy white.

So are the fresh sheets when I
lay my head down at night.

Marshmallows are white, fluffy, and soft.

Clouds are, too, as they float aloft.

WHEREVER YOU LOOK, COLORS SURROUND YOU

And remind you of who you are.

Capture the moment.

See what isn't spoken.

Love each other.

The connection is real.

Oh my dear Grandloves
with your little fingers and toes,
I adore everything about you,
especially your precious nose.

I can't help but cry with gratitude
when I see your glowing smiles,
Or hear your giggly laughter,
that makes the world shine.

There is nothing that Lala and Abuelo
wouldn't do for our loves.
We embrace every moment with you,
and continue to thank the good Lord above.

COMING SOON!

Look for the Hearts

If you look around you,
hearts are everywhere.

Keep your eyes and your heart open,
and they will soon appear.

I usually see them when we go on a walk,
sometimes I see them in the rocks.

Or trees can sometime have hearts upon them
so can leaves, ones of natures poems . . .